20 Weapons of War

Tracey Turner

Published by Smart Apple Media,
an imprint of Black Rabbit Books
P.O. Box 3263, Mankato, Minnesota 56002
www.smartapplemedia.com

Published by arrangement with Watts
Publishing, London.

Cataloging-in-Publication Data is available
from the Library of Congress
ISBN: 978-1-62588-151-9 (library binding)
ISBN: 978-1-62588-599-9 (eBook)

Acknowledgments:
Biblioteca Nacional de Madrid: 11. John Braid/Shutterstock: 8.
Martin Brayley/Dreamstime: 15, 12. Jose Gil/Shutterstock: 17r.
Rafael Laguillo/Dreamstime: 21. Edward Parker/Alamy: 14.
Nikolay Pozdeev/Dreamstime: 9. U.S. Air Force Photo/Jeff Fisher: 16.
U.S Air Force Photo/Master Sgt. Lorenzo Gaines : 13. U.S Air Force
Photo/Master Sgt. Kevin Grunewald: 6. U.S Air Force Photo/Staff Sgt.
Christopher Hubenthal: title, 18. U.S. Air Force Photo/ Lt.Col. Leslie
Pratt: front cover t, 22. U.S. Army Photo: front cover b, 19. U.S.Army
Photo/Tech.Sgt. Andy Dunaway: 5. U.S. Marine Corps/Cpl. Jeff Drew:
7. U.S. Navy Photo/
Lt. j.g. Monika Hess: 10. U.S. Navy Photo/Photographers Mate 3rd
Class Ramon Preciad Presdiado: 20. wacpan/Shutterstock: 17.
Robert Wisdom/Dreamstime: 23. Zim235/Dreamstime: 4.

Every attempt has been made to clear copyright.
Should there be any inadvertent omission please
apply to the publisher for rectification.

Printed in the United States by CG Book Printers
North Mankato, Minnesota

PO 1722
3-2015

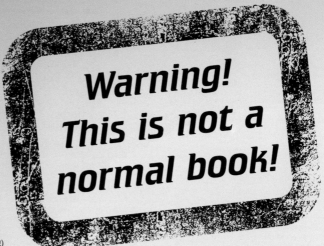

Contents

Please note: Every effort has been made by the publishers to ensure
that the websites in this book contain no inappropriate or offensive
material. However, because of the nature of the Internet, it is impossible to
guarantee that the contents of these sites will not be altered. We strongly
advise that Internet access is supervised by a responsible adult.

Head-to-Head is not just a book that shows you loads of facts and stats about fantastic stuff—it's also a fun game book!

How to Play

1. Grab a copy of *Head-to-Head*—oh, you have. OK, now get your friends to grab a copy, too.

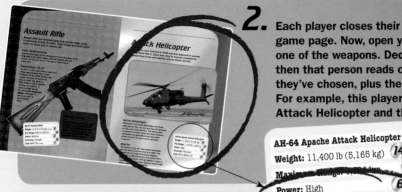

2. Each player closes their eyes and flips to a game page. Now, open your eyes and choose one of the weapons. Decide who goes first, then that person reads out which weapon they've chosen, plus the name of the stat. For example, this player has chosen the Attack Helicopter and the Power stat, with a Head-to-Head ranking of 6.

AH-64 Apache Attack Helicopter
Weight: 11,400 lb (5,165 kg) **14**
Maximum range 2,? ? ? ? km **6**
Power: High **6**
Accuracy: very good **5**
Cost: $30.6 million US **17**

3. Now, challenge your friends to see who has the highest-ranking stat— the lower the number, the better your chances of winning. (1 = good, 20 = goofy).

Player 1

Power: High **6**

Player 2

Power: Low **17**

4. Whoever has the lowest number is the winner—nice one! If you have the same number, you've tied.

Time to flip, choose, challenge again!

If you and your opponent land on the same game page, flip again!

Mash it up!

If you don't have the same Head-to-Head book as your friends, you can STILL play! The rules are the same as for the regular game (above)—just flip, choose a page, pick a stat, then read them out loud. Now read out the Head-to-Head rankings to see whose choice is best. Can a Ferrari beat a tank? Can Genghis Khan defeat a king cobra snake?

Assault Rifle

Assault rifles are hand-held guns that can fire single shots or automatic bursts of bullets. Most troops around the world today use some sort of assault rifle.

Early Development

Assault rifles began to be developed from machine guns at the beginning of the 20th century. The first assault rifle was used by the German army at the end of World War II (1939–45).

Kalashnikov AK-47

The AK-47 is the most famous, and most widely used, assault rifle. It was developed by the USSR (modern-day Russia) and used by the Soviet army in 1949. The AK-47 is fairly cheap to make, reliable, and easy to maintain. It packs a deadly punch, too— firing 600 **rounds per minute**—although it's not as accurate as some assault rifles.

AK-47 Assault Rifle

Weight: 10.5 lb (4.78 kg) (loaded) 6

Top Range: 380 yd (350 m) 14

Power: Medium 12

Accuracy: Average 16

Cost: $600 US (average) 7

Rifle technology

The very latest assault rifles have a range of up to 650 yards (600 m). They are equipped with night vision and telescopic sights, and some have a grenade launcher underneath the rifle barrel.

Attack Helicopter

Helicopters were invented in 1936 and first appeared in warfare during World War II. Since then, they've become essential for transporting troops and supplies, and as attack aircraft.

Aerial Advantages

Helicopters have some advantages over fixed-wing planes: they can land and take off vertically, so they don't need runways. This allows them to operate in remote areas and cities. However, helicopters are generally slower than other attack aircraft, so they're more vulnerable to attack.

Apache

The Apache is the US's main attack helicopter, and has been in service since the 1980s. The aircraft has two huge Rolls-Royce engines, each with 2,100 horsepower. It is armed with a M230 30-mm cannon, and can launch a range of rockets and missiles. Other features include night vision, radar, and target tracking.

AH-64 Apache Attack Helicopter
Weight: 11,400 lb (5,165 kg) **14**
Top Range: 1,120 mi (1,800 m) **6**
Power: High **6**
Accuracy: Very good **5**
Cost: $30.6 million US **17**

Bomber Aircraft

Different kinds of aircraft are used in warfare: fighters, bombers, spy planes, and attack aircraft. Bombers are huge aircraft designed to carry large payloads—usually bombs— to destroy targets such as harbors or even cities.

Bomber Power

The first bombers appeared in World War I (1914–1918). By World War II they had become huge, powerful, and capable of dropping devastating bombs. Large cities were targeted, causing widespread damage and loss of life.

B-52

B-52s are probably the most famous bomber aircraft of all time. Modern B-52s are powered by jet engines. They can carry a **payload** of up to 71,000 pounds (32,000 kg). They're expected to continue flying for the US Air Force into the 2040s.

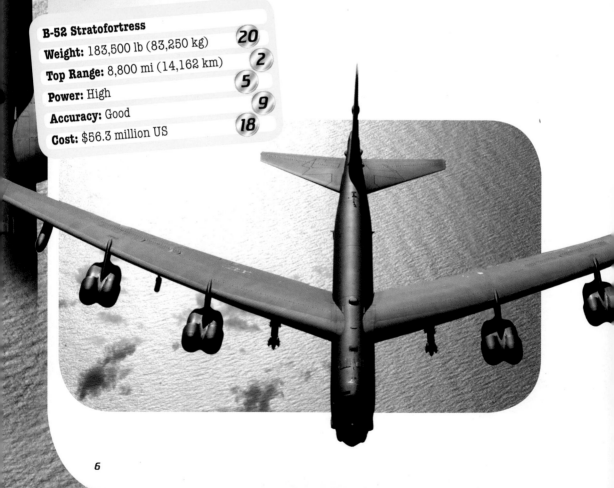

B-52 Stratofortress

Weight: 183,500 lb (83,250 kg)   **20**

Top Range: 8,800 mi (14,162 km)   **2**

  5

Power: High   **9**

Accuracy: Good

Cost: $56.3 million US   **18**

Cannon

Cannons are big guns that use explosive energy to launch a projectile—you know, a cannonball! They changed warfare around the world.

Chinese Origins

Cannon technology spread from China in the 12th century into the Middle East and Europe. There they replaced wooden siege weapons, such as the trebuchet (see page 21). In the 1300s, bombard cannons were about 5 feet (1.5 m) long. They could fire cannonballs weighing almost 100 pounds (45 kg). By the 1500s, some cannons had barrels 10 feet (3 m) long, and weighed around 8.8 tons (8 t)—more than an African elephant.

M198 Howitzer

The modern equivalent of medieval cannons are big artillery weapons such as the M198 howitzer. It has a range of up to 14 miles (22.5 km) and a firing rate of about four per minute, depending on the missile—much faster than cannons of the Middle Ages!

M198 Howitzer

Weight: 15,770 lb (7,154 kg) **15**

Maximum Range: 14 Mi (22.4 km) **9**

Power: High **8**

Accuracy: Average **11**

Cost: $556,000 US **11**

Chlorine Gas

Chlorine gas was first used in warfare during World War I. It is a chemical that causes a slow, painful death. It's considered to be one of the most terrible weapons ever used in war.

Chlorine Gas

Weight: 2.5 oz (70 g)

Maximum Range: Variable

Power: High

Accuracy: Poor

Cost: ??

1
20
11
20
8

Gas Attack

The gas was used for the first time in 1915, when **Allied** soldiers saw a strange-smelling, greenish-yellow mist approaching from the German side of the battle lines. Many Allies quickly became unable to breathe and suffocated. During World War I both sides used chlorine gas, as well as mustard gas, and the even more deadly phosgene gas. At first, soliders used urine-soaked pads to defend against the gas. Before long, troops were given gas masks (right), which were much more effective.

Banned Gas

In 1925, a **treaty** called the Geneva Protocol banned the use of deadly gas (chemical weapons), as well as weapons that spread harmful bacteria (biological weapons). Despite the ban, chemical weapons have still been used in wars.

Crossbow

The crossbow is a mechanized version of the bow and arrow. During the Middle Ages (5th to 15th centuries), it was one of the most successful missile weapons.

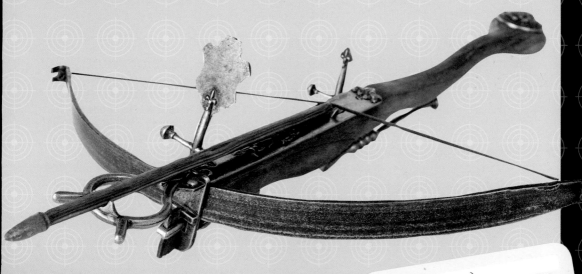

Crossbow (pull lever) **5**
Weight: 5.5 lb (2.5 kg) **14**
Maximum Range: 1.150 ft (350 m)
19
Power: Low **12**
Accuracy: Good
Cost: $450 US **2**

Deadly Bolts

The crossbow is a super-powerful metal bow. Bolts, or quarrels, are loaded and can be released at speeds of 215 miles per hour (350 km/h). A bolt could easily pierce through chain mail at a distance of almost 1,000 feet (300 m). There were different types of crossbows, some heavier and more powerful than others, but they were all easy to use and carry—and highly accurate.

Medieval Crossbows

Crossbows were invented in or near China around 500 BC. The ancient Greeks and Romans both used crossbows. In Europe during the Middle Ages crossbows especially were widely used. They had advantages over the longbow, because it was much easier to train someone to use them. Eventually, guns replaced crossbows.

Cruise Missile

Cruise missiles are flying bombs that can make their own way to a target. They can strike an enemy many miles away, using the missile's onboard navigation system.

Missile Development

During World War II, Germany developed the first cruise missiles: V-1s, also known as "buzz bombs." V-1s bombed cities without any pilots risking their lives. The United States and the Soviet Union both developed cruise missiles in the 1960s and '70s. They could carry either conventional or nuclear warheads.

Tomahawk Cruise Missile

Tomahawk cruise missiles were first developed in the 1970s and are still in use today. They were designed to be launched from sea or land, though today all are sea-launched. They can speed through the air at around 550 miles per hour (880 km/h).

Tomahawk Cruise Missile

Weight: 2,870 lb (1,300 kg)	12
Top Range: 1,550 mi (2,500 km)	5
Power: Very high	3
Accuracy: Very good	1
Cost: $1.52 million US	13

Greek Fire

Fire has been used as a weapon for thousands of years: flaming arrows, hand-thrown fire pots, and flaming missiles fired from catapults. But when Greek fire was invented in the 7th century AD, no one had seen anything like it.

Top-Secret Recipe

Greek fire was invented in Constantinople (modern-day Istanbul), part of the **Byzantine Empire**. The inventor was a Syrian engineer named Callinicus. The secret of how to make Greek fire was kept for hundreds of years, but the recipe vanished with the Byzantine Empire. Today people think it contained sulphur, charcoal, liquid petroleum, and quicklime, a chemical compound that burns skin.

Terrifying Firepower

Greek fire could be put into pots and thrown by hand, or shot at the enemy through tubes, like a flamethrower. It was said to be impossible to put out, and even burned on water. It terrified many of the Byzantine Empire's enemies over the centuries.

Greek Fire	
Weight: 530 lb (240 kg)	10
Maximum Range: 50 ft (15 m)	18
Power: Low	18
Accuracy: Poor	19
Cost: Expensive at the time	6

Hand Grenade

A hand grenade is a small bomb that can be thrown by hand. Versions used during World War I contained gas, but most modern grenades are packed with deadly explosives.

Gunpowder Grenades

The first explosive hand grenades were made in the 10th century in China, where gunpowder was invented. These were ceramic or metal containers filled with gunpowder. A fuse had to be lit before the grenade was thrown, so the person throwing the grenade wasn't always safe.

Mills Bomb

Weight: 1.68 lb (0.76 kg) **3**

Maximum Range: 300 ft (90 m) **17**

Power: Medium **14**

Accuracy: Average **15**

Cost: $34 US **1**

Mills Bomb

Invented in 1915, the Mills bomb was the first "safe" fragmentation hand grenade. Once the ring and pin (see above right) was pulled, there was a delay of about six seconds before the grenade exploded. Grenades could be thrown up to 100 feet (30 m), but the metal fragments of the exploding grenade could be blown 300 feet (90 m) away!

Intercontinental Ballistic Missile

Intercontinental ballistic missiles, or ICBMs, have a range of more than 3,500 miles (5,600 km). That's roughly the distance between London and New York. These continent-crossing missiles are designed to carry nuclear warheads.

Rocket Technology

ICBMs were developed from rocket technology. The first successful rocket-powered missile was the German-designed V-2, which had a range of just 215 miles (350 km). In 1957, the USSR successfully flew its R-7 missile more than 3,700 miles (6,000 km). It was the world's first ICBM.

LGM-30 Minuteman III

Weight: 77,800 lb (35,300 kg) **18**

Top Range: 8,100 mi (3,000 km) **3**

Power: Very high **2**

Accuracy: Very good **1**

Cost: $12 million US **16**

Multiple Strikes

Modern long-range ballistic missiles (like the Minuteman on the right) carry several nuclear warheads. These can accurately strike several targets at once. They can either be launched from land—from **silos** or from heavy trucks—or from submarines. Either way, we hope no one ever uses these **weapons of mass destruction!**

Longbow

Bows and arrows are some of the first weapons ever invented. In the Middle Ages a new type of bow, the longbow, became the most important weapon of the Hundred Years' War (1337–1453).

Longbow

Weight: 1.3 lb (0.60 kg)   **2**

Maximum Range: 1,350 ft (410m)   **13**

Power: Low   **19**

Accuracy: Good   **12**

Cost: $500 US   **3**

Accurate Archers

Medieval longbows were about 6 feet (1.8 m) long and used 3-foot-long arrows. Archers needed a lot of strength to draw the bow. Longbows had a range of 1,000 feet (300 m) or more, and skilled archers could accurately shoot up to 12 arrows a minute.

Hundred Years' War

The longbow played a key part in deciding battles between England and France during this period (even though it wasn't actually 100 years). At the Battle of Crécy in 1346, the English were outnumbered but still won the battle. The English longbow archers were more effective than the French crossbowmen.

Machine Gun

Machine guns are capable of firing more than 15 bullets a second. They're designed to keep firing bullets for as long as the trigger is held down (until the ammunition runs out).

Maxim Gun ("Sokolov" M1910 variant) — 7
Weight: 52.5 lb (23.8 kg) — 11
Maximum Range: 1.7 mi (2.7 km) — 12
Power: Medium — 15
Accuracy: Good — 9
Cost: $6,800 US

Maxim Gun

The Maxim gun was the first machine gun, invented by Sir Hiram Stephens Maxim in 1884. Even then it could fire 600 bullets a minute. Maxims were heavy and took a team of soldiers to operate. They were widely used until the end of World War I.

Using Recoil Energy

When a gun is fired, an explosion inside the gun makes the bullet shoot out of the barrel. The force of the explosion also makes the gun move backward, called "recoil." Maxim guns used the recoil energy to eject the spent bullet cartridge and insert the next bullet.

Modern Machine Guns

Today there are different types of machine guns. Some light machine guns can be hand-held. Other heavier ones need a tripod or are mounted on a vehicle, such as a tank.

Nuclear Weapons

Nuclear weapons are the most powerful weapons on Earth. Their destructive energy comes from nuclear reactions, producing a massive shockwave, extreme heat, and deadly radiation.

Devastating Effects

Nuclear weapons have the power to cause widespread, long-term destruction. After a nuclear explosion, the ground is contaminated with radiation, and people who survive the initial blast become sick with **radiation poisoning**.

Hiroshima and Nagasaki

Only two nuclear bombs have been dropped in warfare. In 1945, to end World War II, the US dropped "Little Boy" on Hiroshima and another nuclear bomb called "Fat Man" on Nagasaki, Japan. Over 200,000 people died and the cities were completely destroyed.

Nuclear Powers

Since 1945, around nine countries have developed even more powerful nuclear bombs. These are China, France, India, Israel, North Korea, Pakistan, Russia, the UK, and the US.

Samurai Sword

A Samurai sword, or *katana*, was the main weapon of Japanese Samurai. Samurai were originally bodyguards for Japanese lords, and later became a highly respected warrior class. Samurai were at their height in the 1400s and 1500s, the Era of Warring States in Japan.

Samurai Sword

Weight: 2.25 lb (1 kg)

Maximum Range: 3.25 ft (1 m)

Power: Medium

Accuracy: Very good

Cost: $6,000 US (average)

4

19

15

4

9

Slicing Swords

The Samurai sword was the most famous Samurai weapon. It was long and curved (up to about 28 inches [70 cm] long), with a single-edged blade. Each sword had a large handle, often beautifully decorated, which was designed to be held with two hands. The sword was worn in the Samurai's belt, and an accomplished Samurai warrior could draw his sword and strike an opponent in one fluid motion.

Scary Samurai

Samurai in their full armor looked terrifying. They had an array of other weapons, including a metal chain with handles at either end, called a *manriki-gusari*; a huge metal truncheon, called a *jutte*; or an iron fan, called a *tessen*. From the 1500s onward, Samurai also had guns.

Stealth Fighter Aircraft

Modern fighter planes fly faster than the speed of sound and are armed with deadly missiles, guns, and bombs. They use **stealth technology** to hide from the enemy.

The First Fighters

The first warplanes flew during World War I. The pilots of early fighter planes fired at one another with pistols, or even threw bricks! Modern fighter planes are much faster and better equipped. The F-22 Raptor is capable of nearly twice the speed of sound—that's a whopping 1,534 miles per hour (2,468 km/h)! It's armed with a cannon and a combination of missiles and bombs.

Hidden Menace

Modern fighter planes are difficult to detect by the enemy. The shape of the planes, and the radio-wave-absorbing material they use, keep them hidden from **radar**. They're also specially cooled to reduce the threat of heat-seeking missiles.

F-22 Raptor

Weight: 43,400 lb (19,700 kg) **16**

Top Range: 1,840 mi (2,960 km) **4**

Power: Very high **4**

Accuracy: Very good **5**

Cost: $157.3 million US **19**

Tank

Tanks are heavily armored vehicles armed with an enormous gun at the front. Their tracks help them cross ground that few other vehicles could cover, and the soldiers inside are well protected from attack.

World War I Tanks

Tanks were invented in Britain and first used in World War I. These "Mark One" tanks took inspiration from an early design called "Little Willie." They were armed with large naval guns and smaller machine guns, and could travel at a maximum speed of just under 4 miles per hour (6 km/h).

M1A1 Abrams

Modern tanks are much faster, more powerful, and more reliable. In 1985, the first M1A1 Abrams tank was produced in the US. It features a 120-mm gun and can travel at up to 45 miles per hour (72 km/h). It is protected against chemical, biological, and nuclear attack. Some versions of the M1A1 Abrams have **spectral camouflage**, making it harder for them to be detected.

M1A1 Abrams Tank

Weight: 135,000 lb (61,325 kg) **19**

Maximum Range: 265 mi (426 km) **9**

Power: High **6**

Accuracy: Good **9**

Cost: $9 million US **15**

Torpedo

Torpedoes are self-propelled weapons that operate underwater, exploding when they strike or are close to their target. The name "torpedo" comes from a type of fish.

Early Torpedoes

Torpedoes were developed in the late 1800s. Early ones could only travel about 2,000 feet (650 m), and at a snail's pace of about 7 miles per hour (11 km/h). A Turkish ship became the first to be sunk by a torpedo in 1878, during the Russo-Turkish War (1877–78). By 1914, the largest torpedoes contained 705 pounds (320 kg) of explosives. Modern torpedoes travel at speeds of around 43 miles per hour (70 km/h).

Submarine Torpedoes

Ships and aircraft have both been used to launch torpedoes, but torpedoes fired by submarines have been the most effective. During World War II, huge numbers of ships were sunk by torpedoes, many of them launched by German sumarines called U-boats.

USN MK-46 Mod 5 Torpedo

Weight: 509 lb (231 kg) — **9**

Maximum Range: 6.8 mi (11 km) — **10**

Power: High — **10**

Accuracy: Very good — **8**

Cost: $1.02 million US — **12**

Trebuchet

A trebuchet is a missile-flinging machine used during the Middle Ages. Counterweight trebuchets were used to attack besieged castles, mainly to smash holes in the stone walls.

Bashing Buildings

Trebuchets used a long arm with a container for the missile at one end, and a heavy load at the other. The load would pull down the arm, flinging the missile (usually a heavy piece of stone) into the air. Once a trebuchet was built, it couldn't be moved very easily, so they were only really used during a siege.

Counterweight Trebuchet
Weight: 48,000 lb (22,000 kg) **17**
Range: 1,000 ft (300 m) **16**
Power: Low **17**
Accuracy: Average **16**
Cost: $500 US **3**

Gruesome Missiles

Missiles didn't just include stones: barrels of tar could be set on fire and hurled at the target, and burning sand was sometimes thrown. More gruesome missiles were thrown too, such as dung, dead animals, and dead people. These helped to spread disease in the town under attack.

Unmanned Aerial Vehicles

These aircraft, also called UAVs or drones, don't have a pilot on board. Instead they're either flown by a pilot on the ground, by remote control, or they can fly by themselves according to a programmed flight plan. UAVs are used in warfare for spying and for attack, without risking the lives of a human crew.

Deadly Predator

The Predator is one of the most famous types of UAV. The aircraft is equipped with satellite navigation, radar, and video equipment, including an infrared camera for night-time vision. It can carry over 440 pounds (200 kg) of weapons, which might include missiles, and can keep flying for up to 40 hours.

UAV Remote Pilot

A Predator pilot flies the plane using controls that transmit via satellite links. He or she relies on the cameras aboard the plane to see what's going on. Visability is limited, but targeting equipment means that weapons can be used accurately.

MQ-1 Predator UAV	
Weight: 1,130 lb (512 kg)	11
Top Range: 745 mi (1,200 km)	7
Power: High	8
Accuracy: Very good	5
Cost: $4.6 million US	14

War Chariot

War chariots are carriages on two spoked wheels, pulled by a team of two or more horses. They were the most powerful weapon of the Bronze Age (c.3300–1200 BC).

War Chariot (Egyptian)

Weight: 80 lb (35 kg) — 8

Maximum Range: 7.5 mi (12 km) — 12

Power: Low — 16

Accuracy: Average — 16

Cost: Expensive at the time — 3

Chariot Team

Chariots were usually manned by a driver, who controlled the horses, and an archer, who shot arrows from a short bow. They were used across Central Asia, Europe, the Middle East, Egypt, India, and the Far East. Scythed chariots, with sharp, sword-like scythes sticking out of the wheel axles, were used by the Persians.

Massive Battle

The Battle of Qadesh, between the Egyptians and the Hittites in 1274 BC, was probably the biggest chariot battle ever. Up to 6,000 chariots took part in the battle. Egyptian chariots were lightweight, and carried two men, making them fast. Heavier Hittite chariots were armored and carried three men: a driver, archer, and shieldbearer.

Glossary

Allied – the name for the group of countries, including the US, Britain, and France, that fought Germany and other countries during the world wars

Byzantine Empire – the empire that ruled lands in the eastern Mediterranean region from around AD 330 to 1453

chlorine gas – a chemical weapon that burns the lining of the lungs

payload – the total quantity of bombs or other goods carried by an airplane or flying missile

radar – radio waves used to detect the location of an object and the speed that it is traveling

radiation poisoning – life-threatening illness caused by exposure to the radiation released by a nuclear bomb

range – the distance that a weapon can travel or fire its bullets or missiles

rounds per minute – how fast a weapon can fire or launch its bullets or missiles

silo – an underground container for a nuclear weapon

spectral camouflage – painting or printing patterns designed to prevent detection by radar or thermal-imaging cameras

stealth technology – materials specially designed to avoid detection by radar or any other electronic system

telescopic sight – a small telescope on a gun, used to pinpoint a target accurately

treaty – an agreement drawn up between countries

weapons of mass destruction – chemical, biological, or radioactive weapons.

Index